EAST ANGLIAN DIES
THE EARLY YEARS
PART ONE

INTRODUCTION

Electrification beyond Colchester to Ipswich, energised in May 1985, heralded the decline of diesel locomotives on premier passenger services on the Great Eastern main line out of Liverpool Street, an era that began during the latter 1950s. With full implementation of East Anglian electric services, further reductions will be inevitable.

A wide variety of locomotive and D.M.U. types have operated in the Eastern Counties; many have disappeared through withdrawal and reallocation, others have soldiered on through several livery changes and can still be seen in the region.

During the early years (when steam was still extant) few photographers turned their lenses towards the humble diesel shunter; we are indebted to those who did, as some of these types are now history along with several main line classes.

The photographs presented in this album were discovered while researching for suitable views of steam in action. The selection shows diesel locomotives and D.M.Us at work throughout East Anglia during the transition period from steam. It also sets out to illustrate just how much has changed over the last thirty years in an area that received diesel power comparatively early in the modernisation scheme of 1955.

John D. Mann, Frinton-on-Sea, 1992

ACKNOWLEDGEMENTS

Production of this album would not have been possible without the help and enthusiasm of the following contributors: P. J. Snell (Frank Church Collection), Essex Bus Enthusiasts' Group, A. R. J. Frost (A.I.I.P., A.R.P.S., M.I.R.T.), F. Hornby, J. A. C. Kirke, D. C. Ovenden, A. E. Bennett, M. Mensing, B. P. Pask, P. J. Kelley, J. F. Oxley, H. N. James, G. Griggs, N. Browne, my colleague Win Cole and the production staff of The Lavenham Press Ltd.

FRONT COVER
LIVERPOOL STREET – February 22nd 1958. In its original condition, Brush type 2 No D5502 (later Class 31/002) stands in a now historical setting. Introduced during 1957, Nos D5500–D5519 had electromagnetic control equipment and Mirlees engines. They were affectionately known as "Toffee Apples". All are now withdrawn with the exception of the preserved D5500. (*Photo – F. Church, courtesy E.B.E.G.*)

BACK COVER
PETERBOROUGH – July 25th 1963. The diesel era at Peterborough. A magnificent study of Brush type 4 No D1501 (later Class 47/402) in two-tone green livery with the 3.00pm King's Cross–Newcastle train. Also in the picture is a Brush type 2 (Class 31). (*Photo – D. C. Ovenden*)

INSIDE FRONT COVER
IPSWICH – June 6th 1959. The down "Broadsman" enters Stoke tunnel headed by an unidentified English Electric type 4 (Class 40). Steam locomotives are still in evidence and the River Orwell is visible in the background. (*Photo A. R. J. Frost, A.I.I.P., A.R.P.S., M.I.R.T.*)

INSIDE BACK COVER (UPPER)
MARCH – May 18th 1962. Steam transition. A diminutive Class J15 No 65420 is passed by Brush type 2s Nos D5667 (31/240) and D5572 (31/154) on a freight working. (*Photo – J. A. C. Kirke*)

INSIDE BACK COVER (LOWER)
WITHAM — March 21st 1959. Five railbuses were supplied to B.R. by the German manufacturer Wagen und Maschinenbau in 1958 and introduced onto East Anglian branches in an effort to cut costs. They were notoriously unreliable and were sold during the mid-sixties. Three examples have been preserved. In this view a railbus (79960 series) waits to leave with the 3.42pm to Braintree. (*Photo – M. Mensing*)

THIS PAGE
LIVERPOOL STREET – November 1st 1958. 1958 was the first year for the English Electric type 4s. No D202 (later Class 40/002) attracts an audience awaiting a turn of duty. (*Photo – N. L. Browne*)

CENTRE PAGES
CHELMSFORD – March 6th 1961. The first order for English Electric type 4s (Class 40) originated from the 1955 modernisation plan diesel motive power scheme. The G.E. main line was their earliest haunt. No D205 (40/005) arrives at Chelmsford with the 11.30am Liverpool Street–Norwich train. (*Photo Frank Church, courtesy E.B.E.G.*)

Copyright and design, South Anglia Productions 1992.
Published by South Anglia Productions, 26 Rainham Way, Frinton-on-Sea, Essex CO13 9NS. Tel: 0255 677965.
ISBN 1 871277 12 4
Printed in England by The Lavenham Press Ltd.

BROMLEY

A magnificent lower quadrant semaphore dominates this truly vintage scene, as Brush type 2 No D5512 (31/012) passes with a freight, probably from Commercial Road to Ripple Lane, July

STRATFORD

Above: The Paxman engined B.T.H. type 1s first appeared during 1957; all are now withdrawn from B.R. service. No D8229 is passing a B.R. shunter No D3835 (08/668) with a tanker train on a very wet day in 1962. (*Photo* – F. Hornby)

STRATFORD

Below: North British Loco Company type 1 No D8405 is pictured at Stratford June 7th 1959 on a Sunday excursion from Hertford East to Southend. The train is seen just prior to reversal. Ironically only 10 examples of this type were built. (*Photo* – F. Hornby)

PLAISTOW

A scene of great historical interest, especially for enthusiasts of motor vehicles of the 50s; these include VW "beetles" and vans, plus new Ford Anglias in transit behind English Electric type 1 No D8018 (20/018) July 6th 1959. The sidings were in temporary use for carriage storage during the rebuilding of East Ham. *(Photo – F. Church, courtesy E.B.E.G.)*

RIPPLE LANE

Another Class extinct, the North British Loco Company type 2. No D6114 approaches Ripple Lane up sidings from the Tilbury direction with an unfitted freight, June 29th 1959.

(*Photo* – F. Church, courtesy E.B.E.G.)

OCKENDON

With tracks partially flooded after heavy rain during the night of September 5th 1958, a Metropolitan-Cammell two-car D.M.U. is reflected in the water during the following day, September 6th. The station had already received some preliminary electrification work.

(*Photo* – F. Church, courtesy E.B.E.G.)

WICKFORD A.C.V. four wheel railcars are pictured at Wickford during September 1953, undergoing trials on the Southminster branch.
(Photo – F. Church, courtesy E.B.E.G.)

SHENFIELD

A down excursion at Shenfield, August 1st 1960, is headed by Sulzer type 2 No D5032 (24/032). Note the absence of yellow warning panels and the Liverpool Street–Southend E.M.U. in platform 2, at this time running on 1500 volts D.C.

(*Photo* – F. Church, courtesy E.B.E.G.)

INGATESTONE

Above: Under converted 1500 volts catenary, Brush type 2 No D5545 (31/127) approaches Ingatestone station with an East Anglian express for Liverpool Street, March 12th 1961.
(*Photo* – F. Church, courtesy E.B.E.G.)

CHELMSFORD

Below: The English Electric type 3 (Class 37) locomotives have had a long and distinguished career in East Anglia. In original condition, B.R. green livery, No D6721 (37/021) powers the 9.45am Norwich–Liverpool Street near Chelmsford on a cloudless June 8th 1962.
(*Photo* – M. Mensing)

CHELMSFORD

The attractive Wickham two-car units were used throughout East Anglia during their short working lives. Being non-standard they were quickly sold, some finding new homes in Trinidad. In this view the 12.27pm to Ipswich stands in Chelmsford station on a sunny March 6th 1961.
(*Photo* – F. Church, courtesy E.B.E.G.)

CHELMSFORD

Above: The B.R. 0–6–0 shunter design dates back to 1953. On March 6th 1961 No D3299 (08/229) is shunting the country end at Chelmsford station. Note the "T" sign indicating the point of termination for permanent way speed restrictions.

(*Photo* – F. Church, courtesy E.B.E.G.)

MALDON (EAST)

Below: Carnival Day, August 6th 1960, and B.T.H. type No D8220 is running round a train comprised of three coaches deputising for the usual railcar due to extra passenger traffic. The G.E. bracket signal is of special interest.

(*Photo* – F. Church, courtesy E.B.E.G.)

CHAPPEL AND WAKES COLNE Above: A Ramblers' excursion from Liverpool Street via Haverhill to Halstead and private extension trip Halstead to Marks Tey and back calls at Chappel and Wakes Colne on the return run, October 8th 1961, B.T.H. type No D8236 is providing the motive power. *(Photo – A. E. Bennett)*

HALSTEAD Below: The Colne Valley Ramblers' excursion leaves Halstead, Sunday October 8th 1961, with the private extension trip to Marks Tey. *(Photo – A. E. Bennett)*

LINTON

A ghost train of East Anglia: a classic scene on the closed section of the Stour Valley line as a Derby Lightweight two-car D.M.U. leaves Linton on a summer's day, August 1961. A detailed examination of the picture shows an ex-G.E.R. ground signal, a lower quadrant semaphore, typical Stour Valley station architecture and evidence of freight traffic. The line closed completely north of Sudbury in March 1967.

(*Photo* – J. A. C. Kirke)

SUDBURY

Above: After closure of the Stour Valley line north of Sudbury in 1967, the station became increasingly vandalised resulting in demolition during 1990. In happier times another Ramblers' excursion with Brush type 2 No D 5537 (31/119) pauses briefly before proceeding to Lavenham via Long Melford to become one of the last passenger trains over this branch. The date is June 4th 1961. *(Photo – B. P. Pask)*

LAVENHAM

Below: Brush type 2 No D5544 (31/126) passes Lavenham with a short freight from the Bury St. Edmunds direction, June 4th 1961. Note the tablet exchange.

(Photo – B. P. Pask)

COLCHESTER (NORTH)

A view looking towards Ipswich, October 13th 1957. A Metropolitan–Cammell two-car D.M.U. employed on the Brightlingsea service awaits its next run in the company of steam locomotives on shed left of picture. The impressive array of semaphore signalling contains starters for the Ipswich main line and Clacton branches.

(*Photo* – F. Church, courtesy E.B.E.G.)

COLCHESTER (ST. BOTOLPH'S) Brush type 2 No D5537 (31/119) in pristine external condition is exhibit No 4 at an open day held at St. Botolph's (Colchester Town) during September 1959. *(Photo – G. Griggs)*

MANNINGTREE

Above: Semaphore signals hung on at Manningtree until 1980. In this view the up Continental boat train is leaving the Harwich branch and joining the G.E. main line headed by Brush type 2 No D5505 (31/005). It is a sunny July 12th 1959.

(*Photo* – P. J. Kelley)

BENTLEY

Below: English Electric type 4 No D204 (40/004) presents a powerful image topping Belstead bank with the 10.30am Norwich–Liverpool Street, June 21st 1959.

(*Photo* – A. R. J. Frost)

A wonderful scene at Capel Station on the Hadleigh branch during 1959. B.R. Sulzer engined type 2 No D5039 (24/039) crosses the A12 with a goods from Hadleigh and remarkably causes only three vehicles to be delayed in the Ipswich direction. The station closed to passengers in 1932; the branch, just over seven miles long, closed completely in 1965.

(*Photo* – A. R. J. Frost)

CAPEL

HADLEIGH

Above: A brakevan railtour arrives at Hadleigh on Good Friday 1962, with a rather dirty Brush type 2 No D5544 (31/126) in charge. *(Photo – A. R. J. Frost)*

IPSWICH

Below: The public debut of the English Electric type 4s (Class 40). Immaculate No D200 (40/122) powers a press run on the Liverpool Street–Norwich route, April 18th 1958, proclaiming "First 2000hp diesel London–Norwich – Progress by Great Eastern". The new machines gradually displaced Britannia Pacifics from the top duties.

(Photo – H. N. James)

IPSWICH D205 (40/005) accelerates away from Ipswich with a Liverpool Street–Norwich train during the summer of 1961.
(Photo – J. A. C. Kirke)

FELIXSTOWE (TOWN)

Above: Brush type 2 No D5542 (31/124) is running round at Felixstowe (Town) after arrival with a summer special, August 26th 1959. Note the basic heating equipment to prevent winter freezing of the water column. (*Photo* – A. R. J. Frost)

FELIXSTOWE (BEACH)

Below: D5542 again, having run round at Felixstowe (Beach) with the same train, August 26th 1959. There is an abundance of semaphore signalling in this view.
(*Photo* – A. R. J. Frost)

YARMOUTH (VAUXHALL)

Drewry shunters were first introduced as early as 1952. No 11103 (later D2203 Class 03) is seen working at Gt. Yarmouth (Vauxhall), August 1st 1958. The loco is fitted with side skirts, cowcatcher and a steam style shedplate (32F).

(Photo - F. Church, courtesy E.R.F.G.)

YARMOUTH (BEACH) Above: Hunslet shunter No 11174 (later D2571 Class 05) displays an early British Railways Lion and Wheel emblem at Gt. Yarmouth (Beach), August 1st 1958.
(*Photo* – F. Church, courtesy E.B.E.G.)

CAMBRIDGE Below: North British type 2 No D6103 then new, on the 5.15pm to King's Cross waiting to depart from Cambridge, May 16th 1959. (*Photo* – F. Hornby)

ELY

A superb study of a Wickham two-car unit arriving at Ely from King's Lynn, July 24th 1959.
(Photo – D. C. Ovenden)

KING'S LYNN

Steam and diesel motive power at King's Lynn, February 14th 1959. On the left is Brush type 2 No D5507 (31/007). The steam locomotive is class D16/3 No 62606. (*Photo – A. E. Bennett*)

HUNTINGDON (EAST)

Above: A photograph which shows that the branch line freight did not die with steam. B.R. shunter No D2005 (03/005) is seen shortly after leaving Huntingdon East with a St. Ives bound goods. Note the Ex-LMS 20 ton brake van. It is June 14th 1958.

(*Photo* – F. Church, courtesy E.B.E.G.)

HUNSTANTON

Below: A busy period at Hunstanton, August 7th 1961. Holiday specials are well represented, with motive power comprising Class B1 No 61363 and B.T.H. type 1 and Brush type 2 (Class 31) diesels.

(*Photo* – J. F. Oxley)

LITTLEWORTH

Above: Drewry shunter No D2302 (Class 03) propels a wagon and brake down the Peterborough–Spalding line near Littleworth, September 28th 1965.

(*Photo* – M. Mensing)

PETERBOROUGH

Below: Another Drewry shunter, No 11156 (later D2237 Class 03), removes the last coach from an excursion which has just arrived at Peterborough, Whit Monday, June 6th 1960).

(*Photo* – M. Mensing)

PETERBOROUGH Birmingham R.C.W. type 3 No D6563 (33/045) and No D6581 (33/061) pass over Werrington with an up parcels train July 25th 1962. (Photo: D.C. Ovenden)

PETERBOROUGH

The up "Sheffield Pullman" arrives at Peterborough and passes the North Box, July 25th 1963. The loco is Vulcan Foundry built English Electric type 3 No D6718 (37/018).

(*Photo* – D. C. Ovenden)

Class 47 forerunner, Brush prototype No D0280 "FALCON" pauses at Peterborough (North)

PETERBOROUGH